Disclaimer

All the material contained in this book is provided for educational and informational purposes only. No reponsibility can be taken for any results or outcomes resulting from the use of this material. While every attempt has been made to provide information that is both accurate and effective,the author does not assume any responsibility for the accurasy or use/misuse of this information.

© Tasos Tsimpoukidis 2017   YouTube Channel: Tasos Tsimpoukidis

Introduction

This book is the seventh from an A-Z series with the goal to
introduce to the kids a variety of skyscrapers
from all over the world.

Lets learn some skyscrapers
and a little bit about their specs!

A is for

Abraj Al Bait Towers

Height: 601m

Floors: 120

Elevators: 96

Country: Saudi Arabia

City: Mecca

Building Cost: US$ 15 billion

Year built: 2011

B is for Burj Khalifa

Height: 828m

Floors: 163

Elevators: 57

Country: United Arab Emirates

City: Dubai

Building Cost: US$ 1.5 billion

Year built: 2010

C is for Citic Plaza

Height: 390m

Country: China

City: Guangzhou

Floors: 80

Elevators: 36

Building Cost: US$ 285.9 million

Year built: 1996

Devon Energy Center

D is for

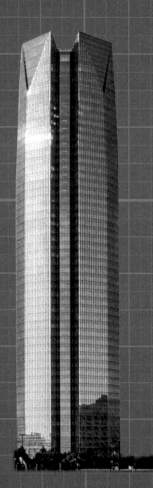

Height: 257m

Floors: 52

Elevators: 52

Country: USA

City: Oklahoma

Building Cost: US$ 750 million

Year built: 2012

E *is for* Eureka Tower

Country: Australia

City: Melbourne

Height: 297m

Floors: 91

Elevators: 13

Building Cost: U$ 415 million

Year built: 2006

Forum 66
Tower 1

F _is for_ _____

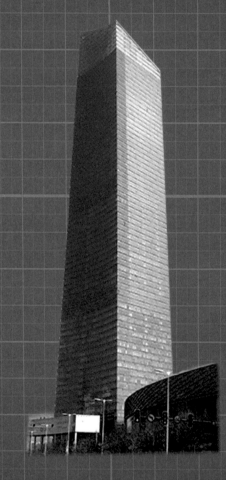

Height: 351m

Country: China

City: Shenyang

Floors: 68

Elevators: N/A

Building Cost: N/A

Year built: 2015

G is for Guangzhou International Finance Center

Height: 439m

Floors: 103

Elevators: 71

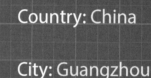

Country: China

City: Guangzhou

Building Cost: GB£ 280 million

Year built: 2010

H is for HHHR Tower

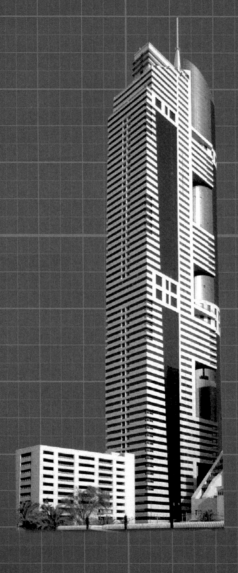

Height: 318m

Floors: 72

Elevators: N/A

Country: United Arab Emirates

City: Dubai

Building Cost: N/A

Year built: 2010

International Commerce Centre

I is for

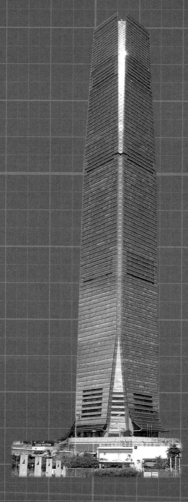

Country: China

City: Hong Kong

Height: 484m

Floors: 108

Elevators: 83

Building Cost: US$ 1.5 billion

Year built: 2010

J is for Jin Mao Tower

Country: China

City: Shanghai

Height: 421m

Floors: 88

Elevators: 61

Building Cost: US$ 530 million

Year built: 1999

K is for *Kingdom Centre*

Height: 302m

Floors: 41

Elevators: 45

Country: ChinaSaudi Arabia

City: Riyadh

Building Cost: US$ 453 million

Year built: 2002

L is for

Longxi International Hotel

Height: 328m

Floors: 72

Elevators: 35

Country: China

City: Jiangyin

Building Cost: US$ 470 million

Year built: 2011

Mercury City Tower

M is for

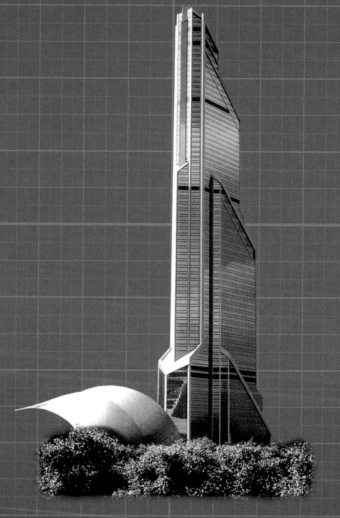

Height: 339m

Floors: 75

Elevators: 31

Country: Russia

City: Moscow

Building Cost: US$ 1 billion

Year built: 2013

N *is for* Nina Tower

Height: 320m

Country: China

City: Hong Kong

Floors: 80

Elevators: 60

Building Cost: N/A

Year built: 2006

One World Trade Center

O is for

Height: 541m

Floors: 104

Elevators: 73

Country: USA

City: New York

Building Cost: US$ 3.9 billion

Year built: 2013

P is for Petronas Towers

Height: 452m

Floors: 88

Elevators: 39

Country: Malaysia

City: Kuala Lumpur

Building Cost: US$ 1.6 billion

Year built: 1996

Q is for Q1 Tower

Height: 322m

Floors: 78

Elevators: 11

Country: Australia

City: Gold Coast

Building Cost: US$ 255 million

Year built: 2005

R is for
Rose Rayhaan
by Rotana

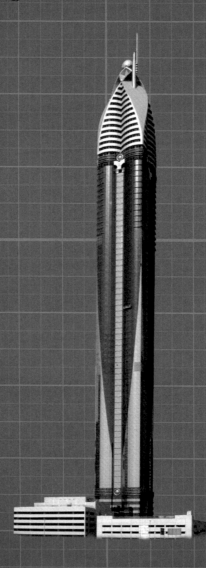

Height: 333m

Country: United Arab Emirates

City: Dubai

Floors: 71

Elevators: 8

Building Cost: US$ 75 million

Year built: 2007

S is for Shanghai Tower

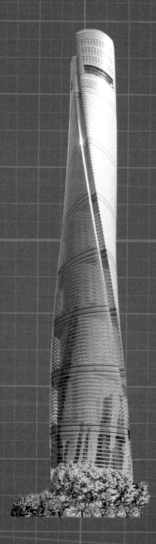

Height: 632m

Country: China

City: Shanghai

Floors: 128

Elevators: 106

Building Cost: CN¥ 15.7 billion

Year built: 2014

T is for Taipei 101

Height: 508m

Country: Republic of China (Taiwan)

City: Taipei

Floors: 101

Elevators: 61

Building Cost: NT$ 58 billion

Year built: 2004

U.S. Bank Tower

U is for ___

Height: 310m

Country: USA

City: Los Angeles

Floors: 73

Elevators: 24

Building Cost: US$ 350 million

Year built: 1990

V is for Vostok

Height: 373m

Floors: 93

Elevators: 67

Country: Russia

City: Moscow

Building Cost: US$ 1.2 billion

Year built: 2016

W is for Willis Tower

Height: 442m

Country: USA

City: Chicago

Floors: 108

Elevators: 104

Building Cost: N/A

Year built: 1973

Xiamen
Cross Strait
Financial Centre

X is for

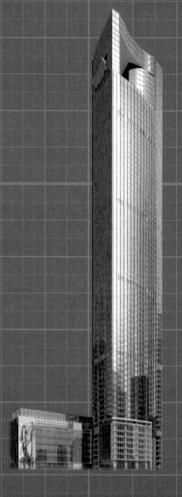

Height: 344m

Country: China

City: Xiamen

Floors: 68

Elevators: N/A

Building Cost: N/A

Year built: 2018

Yingli International Finance Center

Y is for

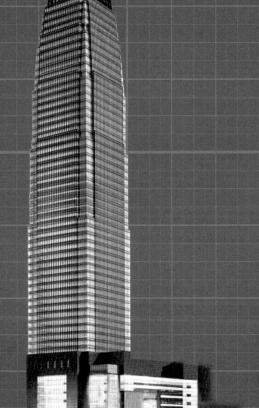

Country: China

City: Chongqing

Height: 288m

Floors: 58

Elevators: 20

Building Cost: N/A

Year built: 2012

Z is for Zifeng Tower

Height: 450m

Floors: 66

Elevators: 54

Country: China

City: Nanjing

Building Cost: RMB 5 billion

Year built: 2010